THE PASSOVER SEDER

PATHWAYS THROUGH THE HAGGADAH

arranged by

RABBI ARTHUR GILBERT

augmented by

FLORENCE ZELDIN

edited by

PATRICIA SINGER GOLDEN

illustrated by

EZEKIEL SCHLOSS
URI SHULEVITZ

KTAV PUBLISHING HOUSE INC.
HOBOKEN, NEW JERSEY

Grateful acknowledgment is made for permission to reprint the following:

The excerpt on p. 52 is reprinted by permission of New York University Press from GOD'S PRESENCE IN HISTORY: JEWISH AFFIRMATIONS AND PHILOSOPHICAL REFLECTIONS by Emil Fackenheim. Copyright © 1970 by New York University.

The excerpt on p. 39 is reprinted from the book AN ISRAEL HAGGADAH by Meyer Levin, published by Harry N. Abrams, Inc., N.Y., 1969, with permission of the publisher.

"The Warsaw Ghetto Monument" by Ber Mark, from THEY FOUGHT BACK, edited by Yuri Suhl, copyright © 1967 by Yuri Suhl, is used by permission of Schocken Books, Inc.

The music for Avadim Hayinu on p. 57 is reprinted from SEDER MELODIES, by Velvel Pasternak, with his permission.

"Passover in a Concentration Camp", from THE YELLOW STAR, by S.B. Unsdorfer, is reprinted by permission of Thomas Yoseloff, Publisher.

Thanks are due to Velvel Pasternak for his help with the music.

ISBN 087068-504-X

KTAV Publishing House, Inc.
Hoboken, New Jersey 07030
Printed and Bound in the United States of America

TABLE OF CONTENTS

PASSOVER IN HISTORY

Passover is a very ancient festival, celebrating the freedom won by the early Hebrew slaves from the Egyptian Pharaoh. Historical records indicate, however, that an important feature of the Passover

observance dates back even earlier to the misty dawn of history. Long before the Exodus, the pastoral tribes of Israel observed a festival of the shepherds, called *Ḥag Hapesaḥ*. Moses pleaded with Pharaoh in behalf of the Israelites: "Let us go, we pray thee, three days journey in the wilderness, and sacrifice

unto the Almighty our God" (Exodus 5:3). When they were refused, the Israelite families offered the Paschal sacrifice in their homes in Egypt. Its celebration in the early spring was associated with the sac-

rifice of the firstlings of the flocks and herds, an offering of thanksgiving for the Almighty's goodness to humankind.

The departure of the Israelites from Egypt during the spring festival vested this earlier rite with a new historical significance. The name *Pesaḥ* now assumed the meaning of "passing over," of sparing and delivering. Tradition has

described it as "the sacrifice of the Almighty's Passover, for that the Almighty passed over the houses of the children of Israel, when smiting the Egyptians, and delivered our houses" (Exodus 12:27). So the ancient holiday of *Pesaḥ* was combined with the newer feast of matzot, or "unleavened bread"

commemorating the emancipation from slavery. The eating of matzot was interpreted as a reminder of the hurried flight of the Israelites from Egypt. "And they baked unleavened cakes of the dough which they brought forth out of Egypt, and could not tarry, neither had they prepared for themselves any victual" (Exodus 12:39).

As the feast of Israel's independence, the Passover was held dear in the hearts of the people. It gained new power when, under King Josiah (162 B.C.E.), the Passover sacrifices, like all other offerings, had to be brought to the national sanctuary at Jerusalem. The present Haggadah includes much of the pomp and ceremony of the temple ritual.

The destruction of the Temple in the year 70 C.E. led to the cessation of annual sacrifices and the replacement of the altar by the home as the center of the proceedings. During the centuries of Roman oppression, when the Jews groaned under the crushing burden of the Caesars, the ancient Feast of Freedom was charged with new vitality. Although the Seder service recalled the picturesque rites at the Temple, the ritual nevertheless served to stimulate the people with hope of new life and liberty. Celebrating it, the Jewish people declared prayerfully: "This year we are slaves; next year may we be free." This dream of a world in which all people will be free and live in peace inspires the Seder ceremony.

THE SEDER SYMBOLS AND CUSTOMS

At the beginning of the Seder everyone sits down to a beautifully set table, bedecked with flowers and candles, and at the head of which is a special platter. On the platter in specified order are:

1. *Three matzot,* in memory of the unleavened bread which the Jews ate when they were freed from Egypt.

2. *Bitter herbs,* for the bitterness of slavery.

3. The *shank bone of a lamb,* as a reminder of the Paschal lamb.

4. A *roasted egg,* symbolic of the free-will festival offering which accompanied the sacrifice of the Paschal lamb in the Temple.

5. *Ḥaroset,* a food made of apples, nuts, cinnamon, and wine, mixed together to look like the mortar which the Hebrew slaves used in their servitude.

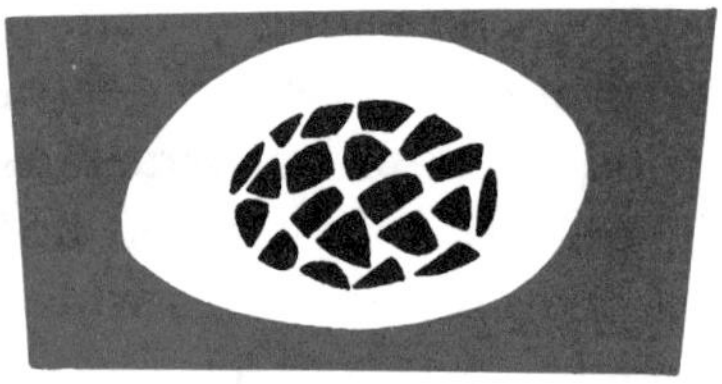

6. *Parsley* or *watercress,* suggestive of the customary ancient hors d'oeuvres. It is now used as a token of gratitude to God for the products of the earth.

7. A dish of *salt water* into which the parsley will be dipped.

A *cup of wine* is set at the place-setting of each celebrant. As in all Jewish ceremonials of rejoicing, wine is used as a token of festivity. If desired, unfermented raisin wine may be substituted.

go to page 11

Each participant in the service is expected to partake of four cups of wine. This number was selected as symbolic of the four divine promises of redemption made to Israel in Exodus 6:6-7.

An empty wine cup in the center of the table. This cup is filled as part of the Seder ceremony. It is known as *Elijah's cup*. It symbolizes the hope for the quick coming of God's kingdom upon earth.

Early in the Seder service one of the three matzot on the ceremonial platter is divided in half. The half which is put away to be eaten at the close of the meal is called *aphikomon,* which is derived from the Greek, meaning "after-meal" or "dessert."

The aphikomon, hidden early in the Seder, is left to the end of the meal. In connection with this, a sort of game of paying forfeits originated. The leader of the Seder sets aside the aphikomon and good-naturedly takes no note of the spiriting away of this matzah by the children, who return it only when the leader redeems it with a gift, so that the meal may be concluded.

In ancient Palestine, the laborer or slave ate hurriedly, squatting uncomfortably upon the ground. The free citizen, on the other hand, especially when there was a feast, reclined on cushions by the side of the table. So it is that in many homes at the Seder the leader is seated at the head of the table in an armchair provided with pillows to symbolize the freedom achieved by the ancient Israelites on Passover.

THE SEDER IS A FAMILY AFFAIR

Because each of us must feel as if he or she were personally redeemed from slavery we must each assume certain responsibilities for our freedom. In order to fully appreciate its meaning each of us must help in the preparation of the Seder and the celebration of the holiday of Passover. Each of us must be actively involved. We must each do something.

In practical matters—arranging for the dinner and the service—every person in the family can contribute. Since many markets are open seven days a week even the working parent can participate in the special shopping which is required. Taking the younger children with you will arouse their curiosity when they see you select matzah instead of bread; or when they see you choose horseradish root instead of the usual vegetable. (One of the primary reasons for the Seder is to arouse the curiosity of the young so that they will ask questions. This gives you the opportunity of explaining the story of Passover to them.)

Someone, with the help of the children, should assume the responsibility of ridding the house of ḥameytz. Then it is time to bring in the special Pesaḥ purchases and begin the actual preparation.

Someone else, man or woman, or both, should prepare the food. The dishes which are used only on this holiday should be taken out and washed. There is a task for every member of the family.

Teen-agers can set the table creatively.

Preparing the ḥaroset can become an adventure in ethnic methods of observance. Someone can research the various ways haroset is prepared. The Israelis have one recipe, the Yemenites have another. Those from European backgrounds have still another way of mixing this "mortar" for the Seder. Finding the ingredients and preparing them can be a pleasant challenge and add to the meaning of the holiday.

Pre-schoolers can peel the hard boiled eggs (with a little help).

Anyone can put the Haggadot on the chairs.

Primary grade children can prepare small dishes of salt water for dipping.

The Seder is a family affair. How far does the family extend? In this instance we think of ourselves as part of the larger community. Our family should extend as long as our table will allow. "Let those who are hungry come and eat and let those who are in need come and join us." The need can be spiritual as well as physical. In today's society there are many, although not literally hungry, who are in need. They need friendship. They need the warmth received from association with other people. In addition to your own parents and children there are single parents with children; there are senior citizens with no relatives close by; there are college students and armed forces personnel who are away from their own families. There are new immigrants from the Soviet Union who have never had the opportunity to attend a "free" seder. There are other immigrants who are newcomers in the neighborhood. And, there are non-Jewish neighbors and friends who are as curious as children about Passover and the Seder observance.

This is the time of year to open your homes and your hearts. Don't wait for Elijah—welcome the stranger now. Then, when you sit down at your Seder table you will see how much you have contributed to the well being of your extended family. You will have an opportunity to answer the questions of all the types of "children" which the Haggadah mentions: the wise (the experienced); the wicked (the one who has been disassociated until now): the innocent (who has never had the opportunity to observe Passover before); and the one who is unable to inquire (because he or she knows so little about Judaism).

Another approach to involving the whole family is to give "assignments" of a thought provoking nature. For example:

1. In what way are you a slave today?
   How can you be freed from this enslavement?
2. There are others in the community who, in a sense, are enslaved. Who are they and how can you help to free them? Or, at least make their lives a little less bitter?
3. What does the bitter herb represent in today's society?
4. You live in a free country. What are your responsibilities to those who don't?
5. Is the Israeli free to pursue his or her own happiness while the country is almost surrounded by hostile enemies?

If there are any children who are too young to participate, or listen, during the service, the discussion can take place after the little ones are excused and/or put to bed. However, there are children, even in the primary grades, who can understand some of the meaning of Passover and add comments of their own.

Ḥag Sameyaḥ!

The Haggadah, which tells the story, is a very ancient text. The oldest portions are at least twenty-five hundred years old; and by the time of the Christian era, the text had already received much of its present form. The whole service is based upon one single biblical injunction in connection with the observance of Passover: "And thou shalt tell thy child in that day, saying, 'It is because of that which the Almighty did for me when I came forth out of Egypt' " (Exodus 13:8). The word "tell" in Hebrew is *higgid*, and *haggadah* means "telling." This ancient ritual, therefore, is simply the recounting of the Exodus to the assembled household in literal obedience to the biblical precept. The Haggadah, however, includes not only the order of ancient ceremonial events and the story of the Exodus, but a running commentary of prayer, legend, and exposition.

Mom

LIGHTING OF THE HOLIDAY CANDLES

All Stand.

As a symbol of the warm glow of happiness which this festival brings into the Jewish home, two holiday candles are lit by a head of the household (traditionally, a woman). Holding her hands over the candles she recites the following blessing:

בָּרוּךְ אַתָּה יְיָ, אֱלֹהֵינוּ מֶלֶךְ
הָעוֹלָם, אֲשֶׁר קִדְּשָׁנוּ בְּמִצְוֹתָיו
וְצִוָּנוּ לְהַדְלִיק נֵר (שֶׁל שַׁבָּת
וְ) שֶׁל יוֹם טוֹב.

Ba-ruḥ a-tah A-do-nai, E-lo-hey-nu me-leḥ ha-o-lam, a-sher kid-sha-nu b'-mitz-vo-tav v'-tzi-va-nu l'-had-lik neyr shel (Sha-bat v'-shel) Yom Tov.

Praised art Thou, Adonai our God, Ruler of the Universe, Who hast sanctified us by Thy commandments and commanded us to kindle the light of (the Sabbath and of) the holiday.

Light is the symbol of the divine. "Adonai is my light and my salvation." [Psalm 27:1]

Light is the symbol of the divine element in each human being. "The human spirit is the light of Adonai." [Proverbs 20:27]

Light is the symbol of the divine law. "The commandment is a lamp and the law is a light." [Proverbs 6:23]

Light is the symbol of Israel's mission. "I, Adonai, . . . have set thee for a covenant of the people, for a light unto the nations." [Isaiah 42:6]

(NOTE: On Friday evening, include words in parentheses.)

Seder means order

THE ORDER OF THE PASSOVER SERVICE

סימן לסדר של פסח.

KADEYSH קַדֵּשׁ. 1.
THE SANCTIFICATION

URḤATZ וּרְחַץ 2.
CLEANSING THE HANDS

KARPAS כַּרְפַּס. 3.
EATING OF THE GREENS

YAḤATZ יַחַץ. 4.
BREAKING OF THE MATZAH

MAGGID מַגִּיד. 5.
RECITATION OF THE SERVICE

RAḤATZ רַחַץ. 6.
ALL WASH HANDS

MOTZI-MATZAH מוֹצִיא .7 מַצָּה. .8

EATING THE MATZAH

MAROR מָרוֹר. .9

TASTING THE BITTER HERB

KOREYḤ כּוֹרֵךְ. .10

A REMINDER OF THE TEMPLE

SHULḤAN OREYḤ שֻׁלְחָן עוֹרֵךְ. .11

THE PASSOVER MEAL

TZAFUN צָפוּן. .12

EATING THE AFIKOMEN

BAREYḤ בָּרֵךְ. .13

THE GRACE AFTER MEAL

HALLEYL הַלֵּל. .14

PSALMS OF PRAISE

NIRTZAH נִרְצָה. .15

CLOSE THE SERVICE

The first cup of wine is filled for each person.

If the festival is on Friday night, begin here and continue on the next page, including the words in parentheses.

And it was evening and it was morning.

The sixth day, the heavens, the earth, and all their hosts were finished. God finished on the seventh day the work of making the world, and rested on the seventh day from all the work of making the world. And God blessed the seventh day and made it holy, because on it God rested from all the work of creating and making the world (Genesis 1:31–2:3).

וַיְהִי עֶרֶב וַיְהִי בֹקֶר

יוֹם הַשִּׁשִּׁי, וַיְכֻלּוּ הַשָּׁמַיִם
וְהָאָרֶץ וְכָל־צְבָאָם: וַיְכַל
אֱלֹהִים בַּיּוֹם הַשְּׁבִיעִי, מְלַאכְתּוֹ
אֲשֶׁר עָשָׂה, וַיִּשְׁבֹּת בַּיּוֹם
הַשְּׁבִיעִי, מִכָּל־מְלַאכְתּוֹ אֲשֶׁר
עָשָׂה: וַיְבָרֶךְ אֱלֹהִים אֶת־יוֹם
הַשְּׁבִיעִי, וַיְקַדֵּשׁ אֹתוֹ, כִּי בוֹ
שָׁבַת מִכָּל־מְלַאכְתּוֹ, אֲשֶׁר־בָּרָא
אֱלֹהִים לַעֲשׂוֹת:

On all nights, except Friday night begin here. Holding the wine cup aloft all recite the Festival Kiddush in unison.

בָּרוּךְ אַתָּה יְיָ, אֱלֹהֵינוּ מֶלֶךְ
הָעוֹלָם, בּוֹרֵא פְּרִי הַגָּפֶן:

Ba-ruḥ a-tah A-do-nai, E-lo-hey-nu me-leḥ ha-o-lam, bo-rey p'-ri ha-ga-fen.

Praised art Thou, Adonai our God, Ruler of the Universe, Creator of the fruit of the vine.

בָּרוּךְ אַתָּה יְיָ, אֱלֹהֵינוּ מֶלֶךְ
הָעוֹלָם, אֲשֶׁר בָּחַר בָּנוּ מִכָּל-
עָם, וְרוֹמְמָנוּ מִכָּל-לָשׁוֹן,
וְקִדְּשָׁנוּ בְּמִצְוֹתָיו, וַתִּתֶּן-לָנוּ יְיָ
אֱלֹהֵינוּ בְּאַהֲבָה (לשבת שַׁבָּתוֹת
לִמְנוּחָה ו)מוֹעֲדִים לְשִׂמְחָה,
חַגִּים וּזְמַנִּים לְשָׂשׂוֹן אֶת־יוֹם
(לשבת הַשַּׁבָּת הַזֶּה, וְאֶת־יוֹם) חַג
הַמַּצּוֹת הַזֶּה. זְמַן חֵרוּתֵנוּ,
(לשבת בְּאַהֲבָה,) מִקְרָא קֹדֶשׁ;
זֵכֶר לִיצִיאַת מִצְרָיִם. כִּי בָנוּ
בָחַרְתָּ וְאוֹתָנוּ קִדַּשְׁתָּ מִכָּל
הָעַמִּים. (לשבת וְשַׁבָּת) וּמוֹעֲדֵי
קָדְשֶׁךָ (לשבת בְּאַהֲבָה וּבְרָצוֹן)
בְּשִׂמְחָה וּבְשָׂשׂוֹן הִנְחַלְתָּנוּ:
בָּרוּךְ אַתָּה יְיָ, מְקַדֵּשׁ (לשבת
הַשַּׁבָּת וְ)יִשְׂרָאֵל וְהַזְּמַנִּים:

Praised art Thou, Adonai our God, Ruler of the universe, Who hast chosen us from among all peoples. Thou hast sanctified and exalted us with Thy commandments. In love Thou hast given us (Sabbaths for rest,) days of joy and seasons of gladness, even this (Sabbath day and this) Feast of unleavened bread, a memorial of the departure from Egypt. Thou hast chosen us for Thy service and (in love and grace hast) made us sharers in the blessings of Thy holy (Sabbath and) festivals.

Ba-ruḥ a-tah A-do-nai, m'-ka-deysh (ha-Sha-bat v'-) Yis-ra-eyl v'-ha-z'ma-nim.

Praised art Thou, Adonai, Who sanctifies (the Sabbath,) Israel, and the festive seasons.

—All recite together—

Ba-ruḥ a-tah A-do-nai, E-lo-hey-nu me-leḥ ha-o-lam, she-he-ḥe-ya-nu v'-ki-y'-ma-nu v'-hi-gi-ya-nu la-z'man ha-zeh.

בָּרוּךְ אַתָּה יְיָ, אֱלֹהֵינוּ מֶלֶךְ הָעוֹלָם, שֶׁהֶחֱיָנוּ וְקִיְּמָנוּ וְהִגִּיעָנוּ לַזְּמַן הַזֶּה.

Praised art Thou, Adonai our God, Ruler of the Universe, Who hast given us life, kept us safely, and brought us to this holy season.

Here the celebrants sit down and drink the first cup of wine.

CLEANSING THE HANDS URḤATZ וּרְחַץ .2

The leader performs the ceremonial hand-washing, but does not recite a blessing.

EATING OF THE GREENS KARPAS כַּרְפַּס .3

This ceremony marks the sprouting of the greenery that comes to life in the springtime. Some parsley, lettuce or watercress is distributed to all present who dip it in salt water, and before partaking of it, say in unison:

Ba-ruḥ a-tah A-do-nai, E-lo-hey-nu me-leḥ ha-o-lam, bo-rey p'-ri ha-a-da-mah.

בָּרוּךְ אַתָּה יְיָ, אֱלֹהֵינוּ מֶלֶךְ הָעוֹלָם, בּוֹרֵא פְּרִי הָאֲדָמָה:

Praised art Thou, Adonai our God, Ruler of the Universe, Creator of the fruit of the earth.

BREAKING OF THE MATZAH YAḤATZ יַחַץ .4

The leader breaks the middle matzah, returning the small half to the Matzah Cover. The big half is wrapped in a napkin or special holder and hidden as the Aphikomon. During the meal, the children search for it. When the leader calls for the Aphikomon, the child who has found it returns it and is given a reward.

The leader lifts up the Matzah and says:

Behold, the matzah, the bread of affliction our ancestors ate when they were slaves in the Land of Egypt. Let it remind us of people everywhere who are poor and hungry. Let it call to our minds people today who are still enslaved and without freedom.

May all in need come and celebrate Passover with us. May God redeem us from all servitude and trouble. Next year at this season may the whole house of Israel be free.

And may all people enjoy liberty, justice, and peace.

The leader puts down the Matzah.

THE FOURTH MATZAH

(In 1962 the baking of matzah for Passover was prohibited in the Soviet Union. After Jews from all over the world raised their voices in protest, the ban was relaxed somewhat for the Jews in Moscow. Finally, in 1969, the baking of matzah was permitted for Jews throughout the Soviet Union.)

As we observe this Festival of Freedom we know that the Jews in Soviet lands are not free. They are not free to leave and live in the country of their choice. They are not free to learn of their Jewish Heritage so that they may hand that knowledge down to their children. They are not free to learn the language of their forebears. Their children are not free to prepare themselves to be the teachers and rabbis of future generations.

As they openly assert their proud determination to live as Jews, we add our voices to theirs. We shall be joined by all whose consciences are aroused by the wrongs inflicted upon these Soviet Jews. They will know that they have not been forgotten because theirs is an indestructible bond that shall continue to exist between us.

We set aside this fourth matzah as a symbol of hope for the two million Jews of the Soviet Union as we observe this season of our Exodus, and we hope that they too will soon observe an exodus from their tyranny.

Fill the wine cups.

THE FOUR QUESTIONS

(A child asks)

Ma nish-ta-nah ha-lai-lah ha-zeh mi-kol ha-ley-lot?

מַה נִּשְׁתַּנָּה הַלַּיְלָה הַזֶּה מִכָּל־הַלֵּילוֹת?

1) She-b'-ḥol ha-ley-lot a-nu oḥ-lin ḥa-meytz u-ma-tzah, ha-lai-lah ha-zeh ku-lo ma-tzah.

1) שֶׁבְּכָל־הַלֵּילוֹת אָנוּ אוֹכְלִין חָמֵץ וּמַצָּה. הַלַּיְלָה הַזֶּה כֻּלּוֹ מַצָּה:

2) She-b'-ḥol ha-ley-lot a-nu oḥ-lin sh'-ar y'-ra-kot, ha-lai-lah ha-zeh ma-ror.

2) שֶׁבְּכָל־הַלֵּילוֹת אָנוּ אוֹכְלִין שְׁאָר יְרָקוֹת הַלַּיְלָה הַזֶּה מָרוֹר:

3) She-b'-ḥol ha-ley-lot eyn a-nu mat-bi-lin a-fi-lu pa-am e-ḥat, ha-lai-la ha-zeh sh'-tey f'-a-mim.

3) שֶׁבְּכָל־הַלֵּילוֹת אֵין אָנוּ מַטְבִּילִין אֲפִילוּ פַּעַם אֶחָת. הַלַּיְלָה הַזֶּה שְׁתֵּי פְעָמִים.

4) She-b'-ḥol ha-ley-lot a-nu oḥ-lin beyn yosh-vin u-veyn m'-su-bin, ha-lai-la ha-zeh ku-la-nu m'-su-bin.

4) שֶׁבְּכָל־הַלֵּילוֹת אָנוּ אוֹכְלִין בֵּין יוֹשְׁבִין וּבֵין מְסֻבִּין. הַלַּיְלָה הַזֶּה כֻּלָּנוּ מְסֻבִּין:

Why is this night different from all other nights?

1. On all other nights we eat leavened or unleavened bread. Why on this night do we eat only matzah, the unleavened bread?

2. On all other nights we eat all kinds of herbs. Why on this night do we eat especially maror, the bitter herb?

3. On all other nights we do not dip herbs even once. Why on this night do we dip twice, first the greens into salt water and then the bitter herb into ḥaroset?

4. On all other nights we may eat at the table either sitting up erect or reclining. Why on this night do we recline?

(The leader replies to the child:)

I am glad you asked these questions, for the story of this night is just what I wanted you to know. Indeed, this night is different from all other nights, for on this night we celebrate a most important event in the history of the world. On this night we celebrate the going forth of the Hebrew people from slavery into freedom.

WHY do we eat only matzah tonight?

WHEN Pharaoh let our ancestors go from Egypt, they were forced to flee in great haste. They had no time to bake their bread. They could not wait for the yeast to rise. So the sun beating down on the dough as they carried it along baked it into a flat unleavened bread called matzah.

WHY do we eat bitter herbs tonight?

BECAUSE our ancestors were slaves in Egypt and their lives were made bitter.

WHY do we dip the herbs twice tonight?

WE dip the parsley into salt water because it reminds us of the greenery that comes to life in the springtime. We dip the bitter herbs into the sweet ḥaroset as a sign of hope; our ancestors were able to withstand the bitterness of slavery, because it was sweetened by the hope of freedom.

WHY do we recline at the table?

BECAUSE reclining at the table was a sign of a free person in olden times; and since our ancestors were freed on this night, we recline at the table.

Performing these rituals, we ourselves taste the bitterness of slavery and experience the joy of freedom. Thus God is made known to us again, in our day, as the Author of history, assuring us that the liberty to pursue happiness, to create beauty, to perform deeds of kindness, to find fulfillment in life are the rights and privileges of all people—and that the task of achieving a society where these goals may be realized is our special responsibility.

(Now the leader joined by all the company recites:)

עֲבָדִים הָיִינוּ לְפַרְעֹה בְּמִצְרָיִם. וַיּוֹצִיאֵנוּ יְיָ אֱלֹהֵינוּ מִשָּׁם, בְּיָד חֲזָקָה וּבִזְרוֹעַ נְטוּיָה, וְאִלּוּ לֹא הוֹצִיא הַקָּדוֹשׁ בָּרוּךְ הוּא אֶת־אֲבוֹתֵינוּ מִמִּצְרָיִם, הֲרֵי אָנוּ וּבָנֵינוּ וּבְנֵי בָנֵינוּ, מְשֻׁעְבָּדִים הָיִינוּ לְפַרְעֹה בְּמִצְרָיִם. וַאֲפִילוּ כֻּלָּנוּ חֲכָמִים, כֻּלָּנוּ נְבוֹנִים, כֻּלָּנוּ זְקֵנִים, כֻּלָּנוּ יוֹדְעִים אֶת־הַתּוֹרָה, מִצְוָה עָלֵינוּ לְסַפֵּר בִּיצִיאַת מִצְרָיִם. וְכָל־הַמַּרְבֶּה לְסַפֵּר בִּיצִיאַת מִצְרַיִם, הֲרֵי זֶה מְשֻׁבָּח:

WE celebrate tonight because we were slaves to Pharaoh in Egypt, and Adonai our God delivered us with a mighty hand. Had not the Holy One redeemed our ancestors from Egypt, we, our children, and our children's children would have remained slaves. Therefore, even if we were all wise sages, it would still be our duty from year to year to tell the story of the deliverance from Egypt. In truth, the more we dwell upon the story of the Exodus, the deeper our understanding of the meaning of freedom, and the stronger our determination to win it for ourselves and for others.

AVADIM HAYINU

(Music, p. 57)

A-va-dim ha-yi-nu	עֲבָדִים הָיִינוּ
A-tah b'-ney ḥo-rin.	עַתָּה בְּנֵי חוֹרִין

A STORY

is told of our ancient Rabbis, how they sat at a table once in B'ney Berak, and talked through the night about the wonders of the liberation from Egypt; so that their pupils had to break in on them, and remind them: "Gentlemen, gentlemen, it is time for morning prayer!"

(The leader recites:)

Thus the story of the Exodus was told and retold from generation to generation. Parents would tell it to their children, that they, in turn, might recount it to their children. But children are not all alike, as our Rabbis discovered many centuries ago. Some are very curious and ask lots of questions; but others, who may be just as curious, are too young to know how to ask. Some are eager to know all about the history of their religion and they take it seriously; others care only for themselves and give no thought to this serious celebration. In all, the Rabbis said, there are four kinds of children, each one quite different, and each needs to be told the story in a different way.

THE FOUR KINDS OF CHILDREN

THE WISE CHILD: חָכָם

The wise child loves Passover. Eager to celebrate the holiday, he or she asks, "What are the decrees, statutes, and laws which Adonai our God has commanded concerning Passover?" In response the parent should tell all there is to know about the beautiful customs and observances of the festival. The parent should also point out that the customs and observances have meaning as the beloved symbols of a great and noble ideal—the ideal of freedom for all humanity.

THE WICKED CHILD: רָשָׁע

The wicked child is irreverent, and does not feel personally involved in the Passover celebration. Motivated by a spirit of mockery, the wicked child says to the parent, "What does this service mean to *you?*" By saying "to you" the wicked child is speaking as an outsider who has no part in the Passover celebration. The response should be firm with the parent saying, "It is because of what God did for *me* when I went out of Egypt. For me, not for you!"

THE INNOCENT CHILD: תָּם

The simple child is naive and innocent. This child would like to know what Passover is all about, but is shy and just doesn't know how to ask, instead saying merely, "What is this?" In response the parent should explain that "with a strong hand the Almighty brought us forth from Egypt out of the house of bondage."

THE CHILD UNABLE TO INQUIRE: שֶׁאֵינוֹ יוֹדֵעַ לִשְׁאֹל

This child, not realizing that something unusual is going on, must be introduced to the story and its celebration in a simple and clear fashion. The parent should emulate the model suggested in the Torah, explaining, "This is because of what the Almighty did for me when I went forth from Egypt."

THE STORY OF THE OPPRESSION

(Each paragraph may be read by a different celebrant around the Seder table.)

It is well for all of us, whether young or old, to consider how God's help has been our strength and our support through ages of trial and persecution. Ever since our father Abraham received the divine call from the bondage of idolatry to the service of truth, God has been our protector. For not in one country alone, nor in one age, have the violent risen up against us, but in every generation and in every land, tyrants have sought to destroy us; and the blessed Holy One has delivered us from their hands.

The Torah recounts the early history of the Jewish people. It describes how God commanded Abraham to leave his country and his father's house and to go to the land of Canaan, where he would become the founder of "a great nation." Abraham and his wife, Sarah, obeyed God's command and journeyed to Canaan. There God blessed them and their family. Their son was Isaac, who married Rebecca. Their grandson was Jacob; and it was Jacob who went down to Egypt.

Why did Jacob journey to Egypt? Because Joseph, his son by his beloved, Rachel, had become prime minister to Pharaoh, king of Egypt. When a famine broke out in Canaan, Joseph asked his father and all his family to join him there. Then Joseph gave his father and his brethren a possession, as Pharaoh had commanded. And Israel dwelt in the land of Goshen; and they were fruitful and multiplied exceedingly.

Joseph died, and all his brethren, and all that generation. Now there arose a new king over Egypt, who knew not Joseph. And he said unto his people: "Behold, the people of the children of Israel are too many and too mighty for us; come, let us deal wisely with them, lest they multiply, and it come to pass, that if there be a war, they join themselves unto our enemies and fight against us." Therefore Pharaoh set over them taskmasters to afflict them with burdens. But the more the Egyptians afflicted them, the more the Israelites multiplied and the more they spread abroad.

The Egyptians dealt ill with us, and afflicted us, and laid upon us cruel bondage. And we cried unto Adonai, the God of our ancestors, and Adonai heard our voice and saw our trouble and our toil and our oppression. And Adonai brought us forth out of Egypt, with a mighty hand and with an outstretched arm and with great terror and with signs and with wonders.

LET MY PEOPLE GO

(Music, page 58)

(The company join in singing together.)

1. When Israel was in Egypt land,
   Let my people go.
   Oppressed so hard they could not stand,
   Let my people go.

Chorus:
Go down, Moses,
Way down in Egypt land;
Tell old Pharaoh,
Let my people go!

2. "Thus saith the Lord", bold Moses said:
   Let my people go.
   "If not I'll strike your firstborn dead."
   Let my people go. (Chorus)

3. The Lord told Moses what to do,
   Let my people go.
   To lead the children of Israel through,
   Let my people go. (Chorus)

4. When they had reached the other shore,
   Let my people go.
   They sang a song of triumph o'er,
   Let my people go. (Chorus)

THE TEN PLAGUES

(The leader and company read responsively.)

LEADER: When Pharaoh defied the command of God and refused to release the Israelites, he brought trouble upon himself and his people, for the Almighty afflicted the Land of Egypt with Plagues.

COMPANY: These plagues came upon the Egyptians because of their evil; yet we do not rejoice over their downfall and defeat.

LEADER: Judaism teaches that all human beings are children of God, even our enemies who would seek to destroy us.

COMPANY: We cannot be glad when any person needlessly suffers. So we mourn the loss of the Egyptians and express sorrow over their destruction.

LEADER: At this point in the service we spill wine from our cups at the mention of each of the ten plagues. We cannot allow ourselves to drink a full measure since our own lives are diminished by the recollection of this catastrophe. We express remorse that the Egyptians had to suffer such terrible punishment.

(Each person spills out a drop of wine from the cup at the mention of each of the plagues, a symbol of regret that the victory had to be purchased through misfortune visited upon God's creatures, the Egyptians.)

(As leader chants each plague, company repeats it.)

1) Dam. 2) Tz'far-dey-a. 3) Ki-nim. 4) A-rov. 5) De-ver. 6) Sh'-ḥin. 7) Ba-rad. 8) Ar-beh. 9) Ḥo-sheḥ. 10) Ma-kat B'-ḥo-rot.

דָּם. צְפַרְדֵּעַ. כִּנִּים.
עָרוֹב. דֶּבֶר. שְׁחִין. בָּרָד.
אַרְבֶּה. חֹשֶׁךְ. מַכַּת בְּכוֹרוֹת:

(1) Blood. (2) Frogs. (3) Gnats. (4) Flies. (5) Cattle disease. (6) Boils. (7) Hail. (8) Locusts. (9) Darkness. (10) Slaying of the First-Born.

Rabbi Yehuda joined the first Hebrew letters of each plague as an aid in remembering them:

D'TZAḤ, ADASH, B'AḤAV דְּצַ"ךְ עֲדַ"שׁ בְּאַחַ"ב:

DAYENU

(The company repeats the refrain "Dayenu," which is equivalent to, "It would have satisfied us.")

How many and wonderful are the favors which God has conferred upon us!

Had God brought us out of Egypt and not fed us in the desert, DAYENU!

Had God fed us with manna, and not ordained the Sabbath, DAYENU!

Had God ordained the Sabbath, and not brought us to Mount Sinai, DAYENU!

Had God brought us to Mount Sinai, and not given us the Torah, DAYENU!

Had God given the Torah, and not led us into Israel, DAYENU!

Had God led us into Israel, and not given us the Temple, DAYENU!

(All sing together.)

(Music, page 58)

1)	I-lu ho-tzi, ho-tzi-a-nu, ho-tzi-a-nu mi-Mitz-ra-yim, ho-tzi-a-nu mi-Mitz-ra-yim Da-yey-nu:	אִלּוּ הוֹצִיאָנוּ מִמִּצְרַיִם,
Chorus:	Da-da-yey-nu Da-da-yey-nu, da-da-yey-nu Da-yey-nu da-yey-nu	דַּיֵּנוּ:
2)	I-lu na-tan, na-tan la-nu, na-tan la-nu et ha-Sha-bat, na-tan la-nu et ha-Sha-bat Da-yey-nu:	אִלּוּ נָתַן לָנוּ אֶת הַשַּׁבָּת
Chorus:	Da-da-yey-nu, etc.	דַּיֵּנוּ:
3)	I-lu na-tan, na-tan la-nu, na-tan la-nu et ha-To-rah, na-tan la-nu et ha-To-rah Da-yey-nu:	אִלּוּ נָתַן לָנוּ אֶת־הַתּוֹרָה,
Chorus:	Da-da-yey-nu, etc.	דַּיֵּנוּ:

4) I-lu hiḥ-ni, hiḥ-ni-sa-nu,
hiḥ-ni-sa-nu l'-e-retz Yis-ra-eyl,
hiḥ-ni-sa-nu l'-e-retz Yis-ra-eyl
Da-yey-nu:

אִלּוּ הִכְנִיסָנוּ לְאֶרֶץ יִשְׂרָאֵל

Chorus: Da-da-yey-nu, etc.

דַּיֵּנוּ:

(All read in unison.)

How grateful we must be unto the Almighty for the many and wonderful favors bestowed upon us! The Almighty brought us out of Egypt, divided the Sea of Reeds for us, fed us with manna, ordained the Sabbath, brought us to Mount Sinai, gave us the Torah, led us into the Land of Israel, built us the Temple, sent us prophets of truth, and made us a holy people to perfect the world under the kingdom of the Almighty, in truth and in righteousness.

THE PASSOVER SYMBOLS
PESAḤ, MATZAH, U-MAROR

פֶּסַח. מַצָּה וּמָרוֹר:

Should enemies again assail us, the remembrance of the exodus of our ancestors from Egypt will never fail to inspire us with new courage. The symbols of this festival will help to strengthen our faith in God, who redeems the oppressed. Therefore, Rabban Gamaliel used to say: "Whoever does not well consider the meaning of these three symbols: the Passover Sacrifice, the Matzah, and the Bitter Herb, has not truly celebrated this Festival."

The leader points to the shank bone and says:

This reminds us how the Holy One passed over the houses of our ancestors in Egypt. As we read in the Bible: "And ye shall say, 'This is the Passover Sacrifice, offered to the Almighty, who passed over the houses of the children of Israel in Egypt, smiting the Egyptians and sparing us.' "

The leader holds up the matzah.

This reminds us how, in the haste of their departure from Egypt, our ancestors had to take along unleavened dough. As we read in the Torah: "And with the dough which they had brought with them out of Egypt they baked matzah, for the dough was unleavened. For they had been rushed out of Egypt, and they could not linger. For they had not made any provisions for the road."

The leader holds up the bitter herb.

This reminds us how bitter the Egyptians made the lives of our ancestors in Egypt. For we read: "And they made their lives bitter with forced labor, in mortar and bricks, and in all manner of work in the field. And in all this they drove our ancestors ruthlessly."

Forever after, in every generation, we must each think of ourselves as having gone forth from Egypt. For we read in the Bible: "In that day thou shalt teach thy child, saying, 'All this is because of what God did for me when I went forth from Egypt.' It was not only our ancestors that the Holy One redeemed; us too, the living, God redeemed together with them."

Here the wine-cup is raised. The company join the leader and recite:

It is our duty, therefore, to utter thanks and prayer, to sing praise and adoration to the Holy One who performed these wonders for our ancestors and for us. The Almighty led us out of slavery into freedom, out of sorrow into joy, out of mourning into festivity, out of darkness into light, out of bondage into redemption. We shall sing the Almighty a new song, Halleluyah!

The wine-cup is set down.

HALLEL—PSALMS OF PRAISE

Psalm 113

LEADER: Halleluyah. Praise, O ye servants of Adonai,
Praise the name of God.

COMPANY: Praised be the name of God,
From this time forth and forever.
From the rising of the sun unto the going down thereof,
God's name is to be praised.
Adonai is high above all nations,
God's glory is above the heavens.
Who is like unto Adonai our God
Who is enthroned on high,
Who looketh down low
Upon heaven and upon the earth?
Who raiseth up the poor out of the dust,
And lifteth up the needy out of the dunghill;
In order to set them with princes,
Even with the princes of our people.
Who maketh those who are barren to dwell in their house
As the joyful parents of children. Halleluyah.

HALLELUYAH—Psalm 113:1-2

(Music, page 59)

(All sing together:)

1) Ha-l'-lu-yah, ha-l'-lu-yah,
Ha-l'-lu av-dey A-do-nai
Ha-l'-lu-yah, ha-l'-lu-yah,
Ha-l'-lu et sheym A-do-nai

הַלְלוּיָהּ. הַלְלוּ עַבְדֵי יְיָ.
הַלְלוּיָהּ. הַלְלוּ אֶת שֵׁם יְיָ.

Chorus: Ha-l'-lu-yah) 8

הַלְלוּיָהּ.

2) Ha-l'-lu-yah, ha-l'-lu-yah,
Y'-hi sheym A-do-nai
M'-vo-raḥ
Ha-l'-lu-yah, ha-l'-lu-yah,
Mey-a-tah v'-ad o-lam

הַלְלוּיָהּ. יְהִי שֵׁם יְיָ. מְבוֹרָךְ
הַלְלוּיָהּ.
הַלְלוּיָהּ. מֵעַתָּה וְעַד עוֹלָם

Chorus: Ha-l'-lu-yah) 8

הַלְלוּיָהּ:

Psalm 114

LEADER; When Israel came forth out of Egypt,
The house of Jacob from a people of strange language;

COMPANY: Judah became the Almighty's sanctuary,
Israel the dominion of the Holy One.
The sea saw it, and fled;
The Jordan turned backward.
The mountains skipped like rams,
The hills like young sheep.
What aileth thee, O thou sea, that thou fleest?
Thou Jordan, that thou turnest backward?
Ye mountains, that ye skip like rams;
Ye hills, like young sheep?
Tremble, thou earth, at the presence of the Almighty,
At the presence of the God of Jacob;
Who turned the rock into a pool of water,
The flint into a fountain of waters.

BLESSINGS

(The wine-cup is lifted and the leader recites:)

Praised art Thou, Adonai our God, Ruler of the Universe, who redeemed us, and redeemed our ancestors from Egypt, and enabled us on this night to eat matzah and the bitter herb. Adonai our God, and God of our ancestors, bring us ever forward in peace to other solemn days and festivals, joyous in the building of Thy kingdom and happy in Thy service. May Thy name be sanctified in the midst of all the earth and all peoples be moved to worship Thee with one heart.

BLESSING OVER THE WINE

(The blessing for wine is recited in unison and all drink the second cup of wine.)

Ba-ruḥ a-tah A-do-nai, E-lo-hey-nu me-leḥ ha-o-lam, bo-rey p'-ri ha-ga-fen.

בָּרוּךְ אַתָּה יְיָ, אֱלֹהֵינוּ מֶלֶךְ
הָעוֹלָם, בּוֹרֵא פְּרִי הַגָּפֶן:

Praised art Thou, Adonai our God, Ruler of the Universe, Creator of the fruit of the vine.

ALL WASH HANDS RAḤATZ רַחַץ .6

(The company recites the following blessing as the hands are cleansed prior to the eating of the Passover matzah.)

בָּרוּךְ אַתָּה יְיָ אֱלֹהֵינוּ מֶלֶךְ הָעוֹלָם, אֲשֶׁר קִדְּשָׁנוּ בְּמִצְוֹתָיו וְצִוָּנוּ עַל נְטִילַת יָדָיִם:

Ba-ruḥ a-tah A-do-nai, E-lo-hey-nu me-leḥ ha-o-lam, a-sher kid-sha-nu b'-mitz-vo-tav v'-tzi-va-nu al n'-ti-lat ya-da-yim.

Praised art Thou, Adonai our God, Ruler of the Universe, Who hast sanctified us by Thy commandments and commanded us concerning the washing of the hands.

EATING THE MATZAH MOTZI-MATZAH .מַצָּה 8 מוֹצִיא.7

(A piece from the upper matzah and one from the broken middle matzah are distributed to each person. Additional matzah is provided, if necessary, to insure sufficient portions for all the participants. The following two blessings are recited in unison before eating.)

Ba-ruḥ a-tah A-do-nai, E-lo-hey-nu me-leḥ ha-o-lam, ha-mo-tzi le-ḥem min ha-a-retz.

בָּרוּךְ אַתָּה יְיָ, אֱלֹהֵינוּ מֶלֶךְ הָעוֹלָם, הַמּוֹצִיא לֶחֶם מִן הָאָרֶץ:

Praised art Thou, Adonai our God, Ruler of the Universe, Who bringest forth bread from the earth.

Ba-ruḥ a-tah A-do-nai, E-lo-hey-nu me-leḥ ha-o-lam, a-sher kid-sha-nu b'-mitz-vo-tav v'-tzi-va-nu al a-ḥi-lat ma-tzah.

בָּרוּךְ אַתָּה יְיָ, אֱלֹהֵינוּ מֶלֶךְ הָעוֹלָם, אֲשֶׁר קִדְּשָׁנוּ בְּמִצְוֹתָיו וְצִוָּנוּ עַל אֲכִילַת מַצָּה:

Praised art Thou, Adonai our God, Ruler of the Universe, Who hast sanctified us by Thy commandments, and hast commanded us to eat matzah.

TASTING THE BITTER HERB MAROR מָרוֹר .9

(Each person eats a slice of horseradish dipped in ḥaroset after reciting:)

Ba-ruḥ a-tah A-do-nai, E-lo-hey-nu me-leḥ ha-o-lam, a-sher kid-sha-nu b'-mitz-vo-tav v'-tzi-va-nu al a-ḥi-lat ma-ror.

בָּרוּךְ אַתָּה יְיָ, אֱלֹהֵינוּ מֶלֶךְ הָעוֹלָם, אֲשֶׁר קִדְּשָׁנוּ בְּמִצְוֹתָיו וְצִוָּנוּ עַל אֲכִילַת מָרוֹר:

Praised art Thou, Adonai our God, Ruler of the Universe, Who hast sanctified us by Thy commandments, and hast commanded us to eat the bitter herb.

A REMINDER OF THE TEMPLE KOREYḤ כּוֹרֵךְ .10

(The bottom matzah on the ceremonial plate is broken and two pieces are distributed to each person. A sandwich made with horseradish (and ḥaroset) is eaten after the leader explains:)

While the Temple yet stood, Hillel introduced a custom of his own into the Seder service: he would put together a piece of the Paschal offering, a piece of matzah, and a piece of the bitter herb, and eat the three together, in accordance with the verse in Scripture: "They shall eat it upon unleavened bread and bitter herbs."

THE PASSOVER MEAL SHULHAN OREYḤ שֻׁלְחָן עוֹרֵךְ .11

EATING THE APHIKOMON TZAFUN צָפוּן .12

(The leader calls for the Aphikomon. The child who has found it returns it and receives a reward. The leader holds up the Aphikomon and says:

This is a sign that what is broken off is not really lost to our people so long as our children remember and search.

Our hope is in our children, to find what is lost, to bring together what is broken, to restore our faith.

Adapted from "An Israeli Haggadah"
by Meyer Levin
(Harry N. Abrams, Inc.
Publishers)

(The leader breaks the Aphikomon and distributes pieces to all present. After partaking of the Aphikomon, it is customary to eat nothing else.)

(The cups are filled for the third time.)

THE GRACE AFTER THE MEAL BAREYḤ בָּרֵךְ .13

(Psalm 126 can be recited here.)

LEADER: Let us say grace.

COMPANY: Let us praise the Holy One of whose bounty we have partaken, from this time forth and forevermore.

LEADER: Praised art Thou, Adonai our God, Ruler of the Universe, who sustainest the world with goodness, and with infinite mercy. Thou givest good unto every creature, for Thy mercy endureth forever.

COMPANY: Through Thy great goodness, food has not failed us. May it never fail us at any time, for the sake of Thy great name.

ALL READ IN UNISON: Adonai our God, sustain and protect us. Grant us strength to bear our burdens. Let us not become dependent upon others, but let us rather trust Thy hand, which is ever open and gracious, so that we may never be put to shame.

LEADER: Our God and God of our ancestors, be Thou ever mindful of us, as Thou hast been of our ancestors. Grant us grace, mercy, life, and peace on this Feast of Unleavened Bread.

COMPANY: Amen.

LEADER: Remember us this day in kindness.

COMPANY: Amen.

LEADER: Visit us this day with blessing.

COMPANY: Amen.

LEADER: Preserve us this day for life.

COMPANY: Amen.

LEADER: O give thanks unto Adonai our God. Adonai is good; Adonai's mercy endureth forever.

COMPANY: Thou openest Thy hand and satisfiest every living thing with favor.

LEADER: Blessed are those who trusteth in Adonai; Adonai shall be unto them for a help.

COMPANY: Adonai will give strength unto Israel; Adonai will bless us with peace.

ALL SAY: Amen.

INTRODUCTION TO BIRKAT HAMAZON:

(The introduction is used when three or more people (traditionally, men) over the age of thirteen have eaten together. The word in parentheses, "Eloheynu" is used when there are ten or more adults.)

LEADER: Ra-bo-tai n′-va-rey ḥ.
רַבּוֹתַי נְבָרֵךְ.

COMPANY: Y′-hi sheym A-do-nai m′-vo-raḥ mey-a-ta v′-ad o-lam.
יְהִי שֵׁם יְיָ מְבֹרָךְ מֵעַתָּה וְעַד עוֹלָם.

LEADER: Y′-hi sheym A-do-nai m′-vo-raḥ mey-a-ta v′-ad o-lam.
יְהִי שֵׁם יְיָ מְבֹרָךְ מֵעַתָּה וְעַד עוֹלָם.

LEADER: Bir-shut ma-ra-nan v′-ra-bo-tai n′-va- rey ḥ (El-lo-hey-nu) she-a-ḥal-nu mi-she-lo.
בִּרְשׁוּת מָרָנָן וְרַבּוֹתַי, נְבָרֵךְ (אֱלֹהֵינוּ) שֶׁאָכַלְנוּ מִשֶּׁלּוֹ.

COMPANY: Ba-ruḥ (E-lo-hey-nu) she-a-ḥal-nu mi-she-lo uv-tu-vo ḥa-yi-nu.
בָּרוּךְ (אֱלֹהֵינוּ) שֶׁאָכַלְנוּ מִשֶּׁלּוֹ וּבְטוּבוֹ חָיִינוּ.

LEADER: Ba-ruḥ (E-lo-hey-nu) she-a-ḥal-nu mi-she-lo uv-tu-vo ḥa-yi-nu.
בָּרוּךְ (אֱלֹהֵינוּ) שֶׁאָכַלְנוּ מִשֶּׁלּוֹ וּבְטוּבוֹ חָיִינוּ:

UNISON: Ba-ruḥ hu u-va-ruḥ sh′-mo.
בָּרוּךְ הוּא וּבָרוּךְ שְׁמוֹ.

FIRST BLESSING OF BIRKAT HAMAZON:

(Begin here when there are fewer than three adults at the table, chant in unison.)

Ba-ruḥ a-ta A-do-nai, E-lo-hey-nu me-leḥ ha-o-lam, ha-zan et ha-o-lam ku-lo b′-tu-vo b′-ḥeyn b′-ḥe-sed uv-ra-ḥa-min.

בָּרוּךְ אַתָּה יְיָ, אֱלֹהֵינוּ מֶלֶךְ הָעוֹלָם, הַזָּן אֶת־הָעוֹלָם כֻּלּוֹ בְּטוּבוֹ. בְּחֵן בְּחֶסֶד וּבְרַחֲמִים

Hu no-teyn le-ḥem l′-ḥawl ba-sar ki l′-o-lam ḥas-do uv-tu-vo ha-ga-dol ta-mid lo ḥa-sar la-nu, v′-al yeḥ-sar la-nu ma-zon l′-o-lam va-ed. Ba-a-vur sh′-mo ha-ga-dol. Ki hu Eyl zan um-far-neys la-kol, u-mey-tiv la-kol, u-mey- ḥin ma-zon l′-ḥawl b′-ri-yo-tav a-sher ba-ra.

הוּא נוֹתֵן לֶחֶם לְכָל־בָּשָׂר, כִּי לְעוֹלָם חַסְדּוֹ. וּבְטוּבוֹ הַגָּדוֹל, תָּמִיד לֹא־חָסַר לָנוּ, וְאַל־יֶחְסַר לָנוּ מָזוֹן לְעוֹלָם וָעֶד, בַּעֲבוּר שְׁמוֹ הַגָּדוֹל. כִּי הוּא אֵל זָן וּמְפַרְנֵס לַכֹּל, וּמֵטִיב לַכֹּל, וּמֵכִין מָזוֹן לְכָל־בְּרִיּוֹתָיו, אֲשֶׁר בָּרָא.

Ba-ruḥ a-ta A-do-nai ha-zan et ha-kol.

בָּרוּךְ אַתָּה יְיָ, הַזָּן אֶת־הַכֹּל.

(All read in unison:)

Ba-ruḥ a-tah A-do-nai, E-lo-hey-nu me-leḥ ha-o-lam, bo-rey p'-ri ha-ga-fen.

בָּרוּךְ אַתָּה יְיָ, אֱלֹהֵינוּ מֶלֶךְ הָעוֹלָם, בּוֹרֵא פְּרִי הַגָּפֶן.

Praised art Thou, Adonai our God, Ruler of the Universe, Creator of the fruit of the vine.

(Drink the third cup of wine.)

ELIJAH THE PROPHET

(The door is opened and the fourth and last cup of wine is filled. An additional cup, the Cup of Elijah the Prophet, is also filled. The company rises as if to greet him. Elijah in Jewish tradition is the long-expected messenger of the final redemption from all oppression.)

LEADER: Uncounted are the martyrs, throughout Jewish history, who gave their lives rather than abandon their faith. In every generation Jews have tasted the cup of bitterness. We are thankful that God has remained gracious to the Jewish people. Those mightier than we are now but a memory, tyrants have been overthrown; and we endure.

From the death of concentration camps there has emerged in the Land of Israel a new life for the Jewish people. Sweet has been the cup of hope we taste there. In freedom, Jews plant their vineyards and build their homes.

Yet, it is not for ourselves alone that we offer prayer to God. It is God's wish that all people might enjoy the blessing of liberty and the joy of redemption. So we invoke the spirit of Elijah. As our prophets promised: he will announce the great day of the Almighty. He will turn the hearts of parents to their children and the hearts of children to their parents.

May Elijah's spirit enter this home and renew our hope. May war come to an end and humanity live in peace. May our hearts be united in God's service, and our lives be sanctified by God's will.

(Music, page 59 ELIYAHU HANAVI *(All sing together.)*

Ey-li-ya-hu ha-na-vi,
Ey-li-ya-hu ha-tish-bi,
Ey-li-ya-hu, Ey-li-ya-hu
Ey-li-ya-hu ha-gil-a-di.

Bim-hey-ra v'-ya-mey-nu
Ya-vo ey-ley-nu
Im Ma-shi-aḥ ben David
Im Ma-shi-aḥ ben David

(The door is closed and the company is seated.)

Psalm 115:14-18

LEADER: May Adonai increase your numbers,
yours and your children's also.
May you be blessed by Adonai,
maker of heaven and earth.

COMPANY: The heavens belong to Adonai,
but the earth God gave over to us
The dead cannot praise the Almighty,
nor any who go down into silence.
But we shall bless the Almighty,
now and forever. Hallelujah.

Psalm 117

LEADER: Praise Adonai, all you nations;
extol God, all you peoples,

COMPANY: For great is God's steadfast love toward us;
the faithfulness of Adonai endures forever.
Hallelujah.

Psalm 118:21-24, 28-29

LEADER: I praise You, for You have answered me,
and have become my deliverance.

COMPANY: The stone which the builders rejected
has become the chief cornerstone.
This is Adonai's doing;
it is marvelous in our sight.
This is the day that Adonai has made—
let us exult and rejoice on it.

LEADER: You are my God and I will praise you;

COMPANY: You are my God and I will extol You.
Praise Adonai Who is good,
Whose steadfast love is eternal.

(Before drinking the fourth cup of wine, say:)

בָּרוּךְ אַתָּה יְיָ, אֱלֹהֵינוּ מֶלֶךְ
הָעוֹלָם, בּוֹרֵא פְּרִי הַגָּפֶן.

Ba-ruḥ a-tah A-do-nai, E-lo-hey-nu me-leḥ ha-o-lam, bo-rey p'-ri ha-ga-fen.

Praised art Thou, Adonai our God, Ruler of the Universe, Creator of the fruit of the vine.

(All drink a fourth cup of wine.)

THE FIFTH CUP OF WINE

PRAYER

What shall I ask you for, God?
I have everything.
There is nothing I lack.
I ask only for one thing
And not for myself alone;
It's for many mothers, and children, and fathers—
Not just in this land, but in many lands hostile to each other.
I'd like to ask for Peace.
Yes, it's Peace I want.
And You, You won't deny the single wish of a girl.
You created the Land of Peace,
Where stands the City of Peace,
Where stood the Temple of Peace,
But where still there is no Peace . . .

What shall I ask you for, God? I have everything.
Peace is what I ask for.
Only Peace.

Shlomit Grossberg, age 13, Jerusalem
My Shalom, My Peace (McGraw-Hill Book Co.)

We, too, ask for Peace. We ask for the safety and continued existence of the State of Israel in a world of Peace. Our fifth cup of wine at the close of this Seder is dedicated to these ideals.

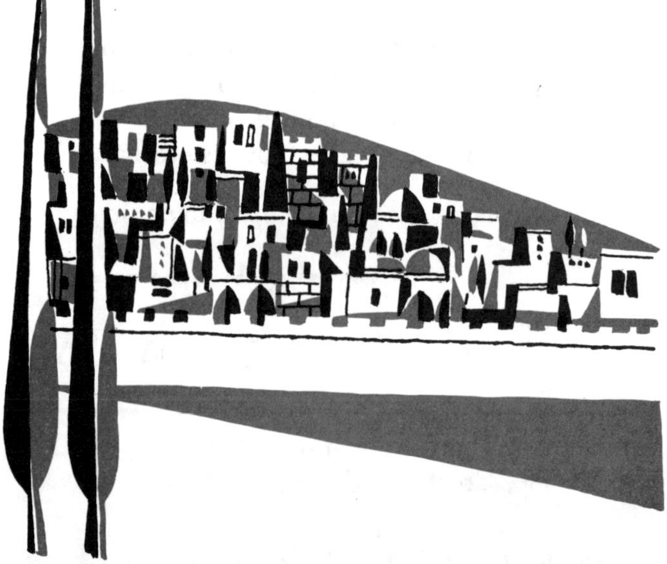

May this service thus performed be acceptable before the Almighty.

This festive service is now completed. Once again we have recited the glorious tale of Israel's liberation from bondage. With songs of praise, we have called upon the name of God. May Adonai, Who broke Pharaoh's yoke, forever shatter all fetters of oppression. May the Almighty hasten the day when swords shall, at last, be broken and wars ended. Soon may the Holy One cause the glad tidings of redemption to be heard in all lands. And let us pray that all humankind, freed from violence and from wrong, and united in an eternal covenant of mutual esteem and love, will celebrate a universal Passover in the name of the God of Freedom.

L'SHANAH HA-BA-AH

(Music, page 60)

L'-sha-nah ha-ba-ah bi-ru-sha-la-yim
Next year in Jerusalem!

לְשָׁנָה הַבָּאָה בִּירוּשָׁלָיִם!

ADIR HU—GOD OF MIGHT

(Music, page 60)

(All sing together:)

A-dir hu — אַדִּיר הוּא

A-dir hu — אַדִּיר הוּא

Yiv-neh vey-to b'-ka-rov — יִבְנֶה בֵיתוֹ בְּקָרוֹב,

Bim-hey-ra, bim-hey-ra — בִּמְהֵרָה בִּמְהֵרָה

B'-ya-mey-nu b'-ka-rov — בְּיָמֵינוּ בְּקָרוֹב:

Eyl b'-ney, eyl b'-ney — אֵל בְּנֵה, אֵל בְּנֵה

B'-ney veyt-ḥa b'-ka-rov — בְּנֵה בֵיתְךָ בְּקָרוֹב:

God of might, God of right
Thee we give all glory;
Thine all praise in these days
As in ages hoary,
When we hear, year by year,
Freedom's wondrous story.

WHO KNOWS ONE

(Music, page 61)

(This is a riddle song that in effect provides an opportunity for a brief course in biblical history and Jewish customs. Children are invited to learn the names of the three Patriarchs and the four Matriarchs and the Five Books of Moses, etc. See answers p. 48.)

(Some children have fun attempting to recite all the verses more quickly than anyone else at the Seder table.)

Who knows one? I know one. One is the God of the whole world.

Who knows two? I know two. Two Tables of the Covenant, and one is the God of the whole world.

Who knows three? I know three. Three are the patriarchs. Two Tables of the Covenant, and one is the God of the whole world.

Who knows four? I know four. Four mothers of Israel. Three are the patriarchs, two Tables of the Covenant, and one is the God of the whole world.

Who knows five? I know five. Five Books of Moses. Four mothers of Israel, three are the patriarchs, two Tables of the Covenant, and one is the God of the whole world.

Who knows six? I know six. Six days of creation. Five Books of Moses, four mothers of Israel, three are the patriarchs, two Tables of the Covenant, and one is the God of the whole world.

Who knows seven? I know seven. Seven days of the week. Six days of creation, five Books of Moses, four mothers of Israel, three are the patriarchs, two Tables of the Covenant, and one is the God of the whole world.

Who knows eight? I know eight. Eight lights of Ḥanukah. Seven days of the week, six days of creation, five Books of Moses, four mothers of Israel, three are the patriarchs, two Tables of the Covenant, and one is the God of the whole world.

Who knows nine? I know nine. Nine festivals of the year. Eight lights of Ḥanukah, seven days of the week, six days of creation, five Books of Moses, four mothers of Israel, three are the patriarchs, two Tables of the Covenant, and one is the God of the whole world.

Who knows ten? I know ten. Ten are the Ten Commandments. Nine festivals of the year, eight lights of Ḥanukah, seven days of the week, six days of creation, five Books of Moses, four mothers of Israel, three are the patriarchs, two Tables of the Covenant, and one is the God of the whole world.

Who knows eleven? I know eleven. Eleven stars in Joseph's dream. Ten are the Ten Commandments, nine festivals of the year, eight lights of Ḥanukah, seven days of the week, six days of creation, five Books of Moses, four mothers of Israel, three are the patriarchs, two Tables of the Covenant, and one is the God of the whole world.

Who knows twelve? I know twelve. Twelve were the tribes in Israel. Eleven stars in Joseph's dream, ten are the Ten Commandments, nine festivals of the year, eight lights of Ḥanukah, seven days of the week, six days of creation, five Books of Moses, four mothers of Israel, three are the patriarchs, two Tables of the Covenant, and one is the God of the whole world.

Who knows thirteen? I know thirteen. Thirteen attributes of God. Twelve were the tribes in Israel, eleven stars in Joseph's dream, ten are the Ten Commandments, nine festivals of the year, eight lights of Ḥanukah, seven days of the week, six days of creation, five Books of Moses, four mothers of Israel, three are the patriarchs, two Tables of Covenant, and one is the God of the whole world.

ANSWERS

(See explanation of Riddles on pp. 46-48)

I know one—God is One.

I know two—Two are the Tables of the Covenant.

I know three—Three Patriarchs: Abraham, Isaac, Jacob.

I know four—Four Matriarchs: Sarah, Rebecca, Rachel, Leah.

I know five—Five Books of Moses: Genesis, Exodus, Leviticus, Numbers, Deuteronomy.

I know six—Six days of Creation. God created the world in six days and rested on the seventh.

I know seven—Seven days of the week.

I know eight—Eight are the days of the Ḥanukah observance.

I know nine—Nine are festivals of the year: Passover, Shavuot, Sukkot, Simḥat Torah, Rosh Hashanah, Yom Kippur, Sabbath, Ḥanukah, Purim.

I know ten—Ten are the Ten Commandments:

1. I am Adonai thy God.
2. Thou shalt have no other gods before Me.
3. Thou shalt not take the name of Adonai thy God in vain.
4. Remember the Sabbath Day.
5. Honor thy father and thy mother.
6. Thou shalt not murder.
7. Thou shalt not commit adultery.
8. Thou shalt not steal.
9. Thou shalt not bear false witness.
10. Thou shalt not covet.

I know eleven—Eleven are the stars in Joseph's dream. The stars were symbolic of the brothers who would one day bow down to him.

I know twelve—Twelve tribes in Israel:

Reuben	Issachar	Dan
Shimon	Zebulun	Naftali
Levi	Benjamin	Gad
Yehudah		Asher
Joseph (Ephraim and Manasseh)		

I know thirteen—Thirteen are the attributes of God listed in Exodus 34:6–7.

CHAD GAD-YAH
AN ONLY KID

(Music, page 62)

(This pleasant folk song describes the unhappy adventure of a little kid, chad gad-yah, purchased for two zuzim, coins, by a kind father for his son. In this parable the Jewish people read the story of humankind ever at war. But it concludes with an expression of hope. Then came the Almighty, bringing peace.)

Chad Gad-yah, Chad Gad-yah
My father bought for two zuzim
Chad Gad-yah, Chad Gad-yah.

Then came a cat and chased the kid
My father bought for two zuzim
Chad Gad-yah, Chad Gad-yah.

Then came a dog and bit the cat
That chased the kid
My father bought for two zuzim
Chad Gad-yah, Chad Gad-yah.

Then came a stick and hit the dog
That bit the cat
That chased the kid
My father bought for two zuzim
Chad Gad-yah, Chad Gad-yah.

Then came the fire and burned the stick
That hit the dog
That bit the cat
That chased the kid
My father bought for two zuzim
Chad Gad-yah, Chad Gad-yah.

Then came the water and quenched the fire
That burned the stick
That hit the dog
That bit the cat
That chased the kid
My father bought for two zuzim
Chad Gad-yah, Chad Gad-yah.

Then came an ox and drank the water
That quenched the fire
That burned the stick
That hit the dog
That bit the cat
That chased the kid
My father bought for two zuzim
Chad Gad-yah, Chad Gad-yah.

Then came the shochet (butcher) and slaughtered
the ox
That drank the water
That quenched the fire
That burned the stick
That hit the dog
That bit the cat
That chased the kid
My father bought for two zuzim
Chad Gad-yah, Chad Gad-yah.

Then came the Almighty, bringing peace
Chad Gad-yah, Chad Gad-yah.

(All rise and recite the closing benediction together.)

May God bless us and watch over us.

May God deal kindly and graciously with us. May God cause all hearts to be freed from the darkness of ignorance and the blight of prejudice.

May God bestow favor upon our country and render it a true home of liberty and a defender of justice. May God grant peace to us, and to all peoples.

Not only must the story of the Exodus be told differently to each of the four kinds of children, but in truth, every person understands freedom differently, each according to the individual need and circumstance. As the rabbis taught, God is revealed to each of us according to our strength. So the Seder, each year, takes on a new kind of significance. For none of us is yet redeemed, and each of us bears the burden of slavery in our own way. Thus it is well to consider and reconsider the meaning of the Exodus.

Every human being must individually discover the meaning of freedom. Thus the Haggadah enjoins all who participate in the Seder, even the children, to taste the bitter herbs and to eat the bread of affliction. But there can be no freedom, either, unless all together in community establish laws of justice. Thus biblical social legislation is justified on the ground that "ye were slaves in the land of Egypt." Freedom requires, that each of us find redemption for ourselves, and that all of us together redeem our society.

In the first of the Ten Commandments, God says, "I am the Almighty your God, who brought you forth out of the Land of Egypt, out of the house of bondage." God is made known to us through acts and appearances in history. Reciting the events of the Exodus we know that God is, because we sense the divine presence in a slave people's insistence that freedom is a basic human right. We know that God is, because history never remains static, but moves unceasingly toward that time when all of us will enjoy freedom from want and live securely in peace.

It says in Leviticus 11:45, "For I am the Almighty your God, who brought you up out of the Land of Egypt to be your God: Ye shall therefore be holy, for I am holy." The rabbis interpreted this to mean that God delivered Israel only in order that they might accept the Commandments. Whoever lives a life molded and shaped by the spiritual and ethical ideals of God's word recognizes that God delivered us from a life of bondage in order that we live lives of service; and it is by that service that we acquire holiness.

The Hebrew people found a reason for existence in that they recognized that their striving for freedom was a response to that which is divine in human nature. Had they failed to open their hearts to God, they would have remained like beasts of burden. Enslavement was not in the bondage, but rather in their acceptance of it. When Moses declared "Let my people go," then the Hebrews served God.

Once one has achieved emancipation for oneself, it is possible to ignore the sufferings of others. Not so for us, however, for we Jews recall our origins: "Ye were slaves." If in remembrance we taste the bread of affliction, we Jews undertand that emancipation for those in society who are still afflicted and oppressed is ultimately our own redemption.

Israel said to the Holy One: "Have You not redeemed us already through Moses and Joshua and all the judges and kings. Yet now are we to return to bondage and shame?"

The Almighty answered: "Your redemption has been physical. It took place at the hands of human beings, leaders who are here today and tomorrow in their graves. But in time I Myself will redeem you. I, who am living and enduring, will redeem you with a redemption enduring forever, as it is said: O Israel, thou art saved by the Almighty with an everlasting salvation." (Isaiah 45:17)

Does it not seem futile to fill Elijah's cup, knowing that the prophet will not be with us? No. By that ceremony we sweeten the bitterness of our finitude and protect ourselves from despair. For we have dared to hope that we are capable of humanity. We have strengthened each other in the conviction that a better world is possible. Thus the Passover ceremony takes on purpose. We recall the events of the past redemption in order to renew in ourselves the faith that God can and will redeem us again.

SUGGESTED ADDITIONAL READINGS

From: "God's Presence in History"
Emile L. Fackenheim
New York University Press

What does the voice of Auschwitz command?

Jews are forbidden to hand Hitler Posthumous victories. They are commanded to survive as Jews, lest the Jewish people perish. They are commanded to remember the victims of Auschwitz, lest their memory perish. They are forbidden to despair of man and his world, and to escape into either cynicism or otherworldliness, lest they cooperate in delivering the world over to the forces of Auschwitz. Finally, they are forbidden to despair of the God of Israel, lest Judaism perish. A secularist Jew cannot make himself believe by a mere act of will, nor can he be commanded to do so . . . And a religious Jew who has stayed with his God may be forced into new, possible revolutionary, relationships with him. One possibility, however, is wholly unthinkable. A Jew cannot respond to Hitler's attempt to destroy Judaism by himself cooperating in its destruction. In ancient times, the unthinkable Jewish sin was idolatry. Today, it is to respond to Hitler by doing his work.

"The Warsaw Ghetto Monument" by Ber Mark
From: "They Fought Back" Editor—Yuri Suhl
Schocken Books
Page 127

On the very spot where, on the night of April 18–19, 1943, the Jewish Fighting Organization gave the signal to commence the uprising, there now stands the Warsaw Ghetto Monument of bronze and granite. About 30 feet high, it is a towering symbol of martyrdom and human courage.

In addition to what it symbolizes, it has a history of its own worth telling. When Hitler unleashed World War II with the invasion of Poland in September, 1939, he was so confident of eventual victory that at the very outset of the war he bought from the Swedish quarries some of the finest granite for three victory monuments to be erected in three capitals of conquored European countries, one of them presumably in Warsaw. He also engaged a Nazi sculptor for this ambitious project.

When the Allied powers smashed Hitler's grandiose dream of world conquest the Swedish masons stopped working on the "victory" monuments.

At the end of the war, when the Jewish Committee in charge of Jewish life in Poland conceived the idea of a Warsaw Ghetto monument, based on a design submitted by the Polish-born Jewish sculptor Nathan Rappaport the Swedish Jews acquired the granite Hitler had bought and offered it as a gift to the Polish Jews.

But Poland in those postwar days had neither the equipment nor the necessary conditions for the construction of such a monument. And so the granite was shipped to Paris, where sculptor Rappaport worked on it, and it had its first exhibit there to the acclaim of leading art critics.

In April, 1948, five years after the Warsaw Ghetto uprising, the monument was unveiled on the ghetto grounds in the presence of the entire Polish government and Jewish delegations from all over the world.

PASSOVER IN A CONCENTRATION CAMP
taken from The Yellow Star by S. B. Unsdorfer
(Thomas Yoseloff, Publisher)

. . . "Knowledge of the approach of Purim and Passover gave us some hope and courage. I approached Schiff, one of the prisoners who worked in the office, and asked him to 'organize' some paper from the office so that I would be able to write a Haggadah for Passover. Schiff gave me some discarded, odd pieces of paper, most of which had drawings of fighter aircraft on the back.

"Each day when I returned to my bunk from a night of work, I spent an hour on my Haggadah. Writing from memory the story of the Exodus of the Jews from Egypt was a worthwhile task. It helped keep my mind off our terrible tragedy and worries about the future. Even during working hours I tried to direct my attention to passages of the Haggadah that required writing. Happy memories were brought back to my mind, of my childhood, and of seder nights at home, when I sat at our table listening excitedly and attentively to Father's recital of the Haggadah which he always did so beautifully and inspiringly.

"Indeed, this work served as a source of great courage and hope for me. It was a reminder that our people have gone through many difficult and tragic experiences in our long history, and have been freed each time, by the will of God, from bondage and slavery. How wise, I thought, of our great rabbis of the past to command that the stories of Passover and Purim be repeated each year, and thus remain alive among the Jewish people. Where would we have gained the courage and strength to survive all our sufferings, were it not for our great and historic past?

"Yes, I felt Passover ought to be celebrated in the camp, and not just by reciting the Haggadah, but also by eating the traditional matzoth. I went to the foreman who worked on the tool bench, a quiet man who had been kind to me in the past. 'Herr Overseer,' I said, 'I want to ask you a very great favor.'

" 'What is it?' he looked surprised.

" 'Nothing dreadful,' I assured him hastily. 'I want you to please bring me half a pound of plain flour, which I need badly. I beg you.' "

" 'Flour? What the devil for? Birthday cake?' he smiled sarcastically.

" 'For a purely religious purpose,' I explained. 'No one will ever know it came from you. There is no one else I can turn to.'

"He looked cautious. 'Things are hard nowadays, the guards are strict in their inspections, and the atmosphere is tense. I can't promise.'

"What he said was true. Besides the raw material and transportation difficulties, ever-increasing air raid alarms reduced our working time to a few hours per shift. We knew that in a matter of weeks, or possibly days, great changes would take place. The factory would have to close, and we would either be liberated or transported elsewhere to be killed. At the back of our minds we hoped we would still be at Nieder-Orschel when the first American tank bulldozed its way into the village.

"On Saturday morning, just before Passover, the civilian employees of the camp collected their personal belongings, since they were leaving camp because of lack of work. In the rush, the friendly overseer came to me as I did the final cleaning of my machine.

"He pushed a small bag of flour into my pocket and whispered: 'We shan't be coming here anymore. I brought you the flour and good luck.'

"I was pleased. 'If we are to get the matzoth made,' I said to my friend, Benzi, who was our leader, 'it must be done this evening immediately after the Sabbath, otherwise we shall have no fire for baking.'

"So at the end of Sabbath, Grunwald, Fischof, and I sneaked out of the barrack and into the smithy's workshop. Fischof worked desperately at the bellows to liven the dying embers. Grunwald worked hastily on the dough, while I cleaned up a dirty tin plate to serve as a platter.

"Withing half an hour, three tiny round matzoth were taking shape and color, accompanied by our happy murmer that these matzoth were being prepared for the sake of God and His commandments.

"Nothing was as soothing and satisfying as the knowledge that even in this God-forsaken death camp, where the value of a cigarette was greater than a life—even here, three little matzoth had been baked in preparation of the forthcoming Passover festival.

"There were tears in the eyes of every one of the eighty inmates in Room 10, when after nightfall on Wednesday, March 28th, 1945, I opened my little hand written Haggadah, lifted up the three little matzoth, and recited the first chapter, beginning with the familiar opening words 'Lo, this is the bread of affliction which our forefathers ate in the land of Egypt. Let all who are hungry come and feast with us! This year we are here, next year may we be in Jerusalem. This year we are slaves, next year we shall be free men!'

"Everyone came to our table. Rabbi Domany, a little old man from Hungary who lived in the next room, was asked to sit at the head of the table and conduct the seder. I read the passages from the Haggadah as loudly as I dared, and the rest followed in a whisper. The, raising a rusty cup of black coffee which he had saved from the morning in place of the traditional cup of red wine, Rabbi Domany called out in a tear-choked voice the words of the Haggadah:

> And it is this promise which has stood by our ancestors and by us. For it was not just one person who rose up against us to destroy us, but in every generation men rise against us. But the Holy One, Blessed be He, delivers us from their hand.

"How true were the words that evening. Never before have so many men at one and the same time been so overawed in their trust of Almight God as on that evening in Room 10 at Nieder-Orschel; never before was there such a truly solemn seder service; never before was there such a longing for God and His protective arm."

PASSOVER MUSIC

AVADIM HAYINU

(p.22)

No capo

Allegro

LET MY PEOPLE GO

Capo 3rd (play Em)

Moderately slow

(p.28)

Spiritual

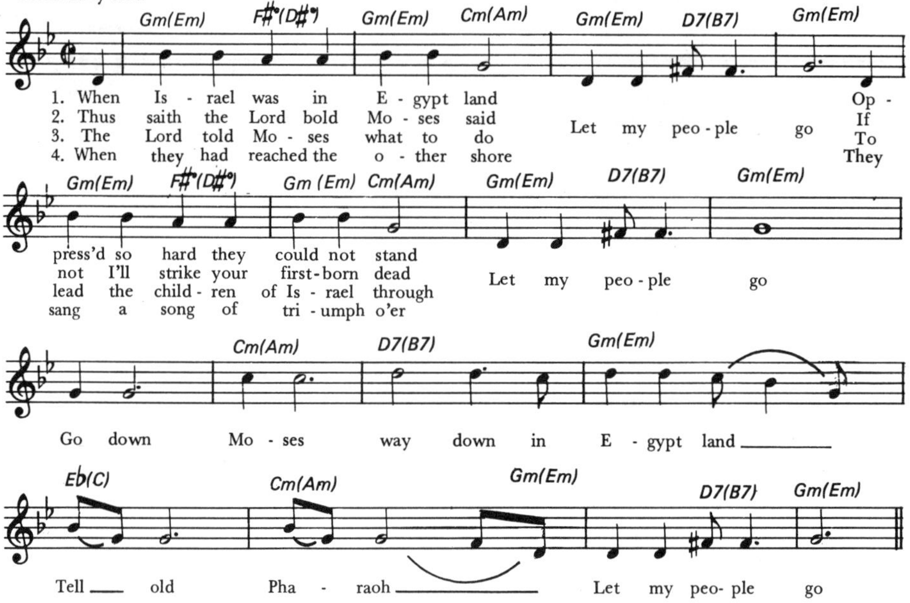
Gm(Em) F♯°(D♯°) Gm(Em) Cm(Am) Gm(Em) D7(B7) Gm(Em)
1. When Is - rael was in E - gypt land Let my peo - ple go Op -
2. Thus saith the Lord bold Mo - ses said Let my peo - ple go If
3. The Lord told Mo - ses what to do Let my peo - ple go To
4. When they had reached the o - ther shore Let my peo - ple go They
Gm(Em) F♯°(D♯°) Gm (Em) Cm(Am) Gm(Em) D7(B7) Gm(Em)
press'd so hard they could not stand Let my peo - ple go
not I'll strike your first-born dead
lead the child - ren of Is - rael through
sang a song of tri - umph o'er
Cm(Am) D7(B7) Gm(Em)
Go down Mo - ses way down in E - gypt land
Eb(C) Cm(Am) Gm(Em) D7(B7) Gm(Em)
Tell old Pha - raoh Let my peo- ple go

DAYENU

No capo

Lively

(p.30)

Folksong

D A7 D
Da - da - ye - nu da - da - ye - nu
A7 1. D 2. D
da - da - ye - nu da - ye - nu da - ye - nu da - ye - nu ye - nu da - ye - nu
D A7 D A7
1. I - lu ho - tzi ho - tzi - a - nu ho - tzi - a - nu mi - mitz - ra - yim
2. I - lu na - tan na - tan la - nu na - tan la - nu et ha - sha - bat
3. I - lu na - tan na - tan la - nu ná - tan la - nu et ha - to - ra
4. I - lu hich - ni hich - ni - sa - nu hich - ni - sa - nu l'eretz Yis - ra - el
D A7 D A7 D A7 D
ho - tzi - a - nu mi - mitz - ra - yim Da - ye - nu
na - tan la - nu et ha - sha - bat Da - ye - nu
na - tan la - nu et ha - to - ra Da - ye - nu
hich - ni - sa - nu l'eretz Yis - ra - el Da - ye - nu

HALLELUYAH

Capo 3rd (play Em)

Joyfully

(p.34)

Israeli

ELIYAHU HANAVI

Capo 1st (Play Em)

(p.42)

Folksong

L'SHANA HABA—A

Capo: 5th (begin on A)

Joyfully and rhythmically

(p.45)

Moshe Nathanson

D (A)
L' sha - na ha - ba - a l' - sha - na ha - ba - a
D(A) Cm(Gm) D(A)
l' - sha - na ha - ba - a bi - ru - sha - la - yim
Gm(Dm) Cm(Gm) D(A)
l' - sha - na ha - ba - a
Gm(Dm) Cm(Gm) D(A)
l' - sha - na ha - ba - a bi - ru -sha - la - yim
D(A)
l' - sha - na ha - ba - a l' - sha - na ha - ba - a
Cm(Gm) D(A)
bi - ru - sha - la - yim

GOD OF MIGHT/ADIR HU

Capo 3rd (play G)

Moderately bright

(p.46)

Traditional

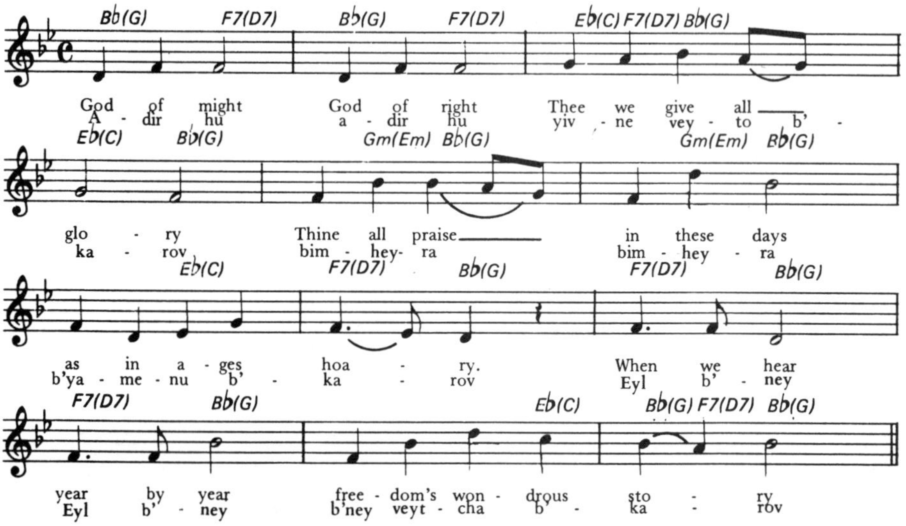
Bb(G) F7(D7) Bb(G) F7(D7) Eb(C) F7(D7) Bb(G)
God of might God of right Thee we give all
A - dir hu a - dir hu yiv - ne vey - to b' -
Eb(C) Bb(G) Gm(Em) Bb(G) Gm(Em) Bb(G)
glo - ry Thine all praise in these days
ka - rov bim - hey- ra bim - hey - ra
Eb(C) F7(D7) Bb(G) F7(D7) Bb(G)
as in a - ges hoa - ry. When we hear
b'ya - me - nu b' - ka - rov Eyl b' - ney
F7(D7) Bb(G) Eb(C) Bb(G) F7(D7) Bb(G)
year by year free - dom's won - drous sto - ry
Eyl b' - ney b'ney veyt - cha b' - ka - rov

EHAD MI YODEA—WHO KNOWS ONE?

(pp.46-48)

No capo

Continue in the same manner with numbers 5 through 13

CHAD GADYAH

No capo

(pp.49-50)

Folk tune

hit the dog that bit the cat that chased the kid
My fa - ther bought for two zu - zim chad gad - ya
4. Fire
accelerando
chad gad - yah. Then came the fire and burned the stick that
hit the dog that bit the cat that chased the kid
My fa - ther bought for two zu - zim chad gad - yah
5. Water
a tempo
chad gad - yah. Then came the wa - ter and quenched the fire that
accelerando
burned the stick that hit the dog that bit the cat that
chased the kid. My fa - ther bought for two zu - zim
Repeat the melody with No. 6 Ox, No. 7 Shochet
8. The Almighty
Slowly
chad gad - yah chad gad - yah. Then came The Al - migh - ty
rit. molto
bring - ing peace chad gad - ya chad gad - yah.